Everything l
with Orange

Derek Dohren

Black Eyes Publishing UK

Everything Rhymes with Orange
By Derek Dohren
© Derek Dohren, 2019

Published by Black Eyes Publishing UK, 2019
Brockworth, Gloucestershire, England
www.blackeyespublishinguk.co.uk

ISBN: 978-1-913195-03-8

Derek Dohren has asserted his moral right under the Copyright, Designs and Patents Act, 1988, to be identified as the author of this work.

A CIP catalogue record for this title is available from the British Library.

Front Cover Picture: Pelágia Pais, Intuitive Guide and Artist
www.pelagiapais.com

Cover design: Jason Conway, cre8urbrand.
www.cre8urbrand.co.uk

Dedicated with love, to my mum.

Contents

Notes

Versions of *Isabel* and *Infinitely Yours* first appeared in *The Cats of the River Darro*, ISBN-13 978-1478315537, by the same author.

Make it Stop was first published in *Further Within Darkness and Light*, ISBN-13 978-1986671675, a poetry collection compiled by Paul B Morris.

Introduction

It has never been my intention to tell anyone how they should or shouldn't interpret my work. That is the sole preserve of you, the reader. It is a philosophy I take with me from my efforts as a painter.

The reward is that I'm often pleasantly surprised to hear what catches the attention of those who stop to look or listen. It's humbling to receive that insight and wisdom.

Occasionally I'm shocked to have missed something profound in my work that is subsequently made obvious to me and of course, from time to time it's uncomfortable to receive a scathing critique!

No matter.

Whichever way the feedback falls it seems to me that handing out prior clues and guidelines to how a piece of creative work should be understood restricts the possibilities of what a viewer, a reader or a listener may otherwise experience. Nobody needs to be told what to think, or what to feel.

In that spirit I cordially invite you to browse the poems in this book as you see fit, and to make of them what you will.

Whatever thoughts and emotions they foster, will be properly your own.

Derek Dohren, June 2019.

Did We Ever?

Did you ever read that letter I never wrote?
I wonder if you ever will or if you won't
After not writing it I never sent it to you
You never knew what I didn't go through
I didn't feel the pain I never expressed
There is no heaviness I never got off my chest.

Did I never believe that you ever existed?
You wonder if I ever did or if I didn't
After not being there you never fell apart
I never knew I didn't break your heart
You didn't lose the time you never laid aside
There is no heaviness you never got to hide.

Make it Stop

Bathroom singer, ringer of fingertips
flinger of fingerprint tips
silicon chipped, lipo-sucked lips
full fat fried fish and chips.
Glutton dressed as mutton.
Consumer whore wrought
and store-bought, with malice aforethought.
Effervescent omnipresence.
Built-in obsolescence.

This international race
and national disgrace.
Face palm, microphone drop
someone's gotta make it stop.

Subsumed consumer, consummate seducer
medically induced assumer
producer of intruding tumours
reducer of humorous juices.
Genuflect and resurrect
a circumspect Jesuit
reflect back onto it, a deflecting conduit.
Inevitable complicity.
Irrevocable duplicity.

This international race
and national disgrace.
Face palm, microphone drop
someone's gotta make it stop.

Concealing appeaser, appealing teaser
squeezer and seizing policer
freezer of wheezy sneezing
healer of needy feeling.
Contactless interaction
contracted spinal column
a cosmic microcosm of global oppression.

Victims of circumstance
of unhappy happenstance.

This international race
and national disgrace.
Face palm, microphone drop
someone's gotta make it stop.

The Man with the Negative Charisma

The man with the negative charisma
sure ain't one of life's experimenters.
I see him now and then buying pizza
I bet he darkens every room he enters.

Someone told me he was married once.
Now he makes no impression on life
and largely avoids bars and restaurants.
He don't need no one, don't need a wife.

His colour of choice of course, is grey.
Aye, he'll say "good morning" as he passes
but really, he's got nothing much to say
blinking behind his plastic glasses.

His name in the Book of Life's a misprint.
His face on the page a dreadful gaffe.
He goes through life leaving only footprints
while taking lonely photographs.

Though you'd notice no absence of gaiety
if he disappeared in holy ascension
to another world, perhaps he's a deity
vibrating in some wonderful dimension.

And wouldn't that be a kick in the head
if that's where he swooshed to every night
while you lay unconscious in your bed
dribbling under the waxing moonlight.

Everything Rhymes with Orange

Either side of breakfast
exciting ideas formed.
A decision to do something truly extraordinary
next August
which would result in a best-selling book
details to be confirmed
and a plan to paint the living room walls
a mish mash of vibrant primary colours.
Such grand thoughts come in threes.
On the way home from the café
while musing on the living room thing
the dawning of a realisation
that orange was his favourite colour.
An epiphany delivered with a nagging price.
How much time had been wasted not knowing?
Should he just paint
all the living room walls orange then?
And would August's great adventure
have at its heart
the colour orange
or God forbid, the fruit?

Breakfast itself had been a failure.
A café he'd not been to before.
Ignored by the waitress.
when it finally arrived
the orange juice came with pulpy bits.
It was all karma for being rude
to that gypsy woman
at the cathedral the day before.
He should've bought the lucky heather
and thanked her
instead of telling her to sod off
which hadn't been as exhilarating
as anticipated.
Karma does as karma will
and serves you right he thought.

The edge off the morning's revelations
taken by guilt
and a disastrous breakfast.
The two were linked
but back to August's great adventure
and the best-selling book!

That's what needed focus
or maybe the living room project
was more urgent
not to say slightly more realistic.
But it was no use
every time he tried to think
he saw the gypsy woman's orange face.
Unless he sought out the old hag
and apologized
nothing would progress.
Buy the dreadful heather
or whatever weed it was
toss it straight in the bin afterwards
when she wasn't looking.
Karma would meet him half-way
he was sure of that.
He finished his banana
put on his orange training shoes
and grabbed his jacket.
How much time had been wasted
not knowing?

Traces

I'd never considered the sense of loss
my thoughts focused on being commercial
selling as many pictures as I could.
It never entered my head that I viewed
each completed work as a child
imbued with my own DNA.
Yes, you want them to spread their wings;
fly the nest, but departure is painful.
To win
I have to learn how to lose

So, to compensate I search for traces.
For instance, those flecks of cerulean blue
on the arm of my glasses, that once
coloured my Galician landscape
and that little blob of lemon yellow
still lingering on my laptop mouse
from when I painted the portrait
of the flamenco dancer.
To lose
I have to learn how to die

In a jiffy bag jealously guarded
outline sketches of a wonderful abstract
I poured my soul into.
The buyer could see what I could see
and that gave me comfort
but I only have finite resources.
Each time it happens
a little piece of me is taken.
To die
I have to learn how to live.

India

India works
in a Worcestershire cattery.
Thirty-nine, but in the wind chill
that feels like flattery.
She upscales her furniture
and kneads her own dough
practices good karma
and has a serviceable libido.

A vegetarian-humanitarian
environmentally predisposed
but she won't go vegan
'cos she loves her cheese on toast.
She's also into leather sports
says it keeps her thin
she's not gluten free
though she's got glowing skin.

Drinks a lot of herbal tea
got rid of her double chin
loves a kale smoothie
and has a balanced yang and yin.
And though she's much maligned
perhaps a little manic
her chakras are aligned
she's gone fully organic.

India undergoes
past life regression hypnosis.
Multiple lives, but in the wind chill
that feels like psychosis.
She was once a handmaiden
of Marie Antionette
and helped built a monastery
in remotest Tibet.

But when she was a man
he was often quite mad
in 44 BC stabbed
Julius Caesar real bad.
Fought with Atilla the Hun
and with Vlad the Impaler
and as a pirate at sea
he made a fearsome sailor.

Her watch is right to the second
but not to the hour.
The amaryllis mum bought her
is yet to flower.
But she's gonna live forever
she goes in for all that Zen.
Puts it down to mindfulness
again and again and again.

India likes
a little Motown; enjoys a bit of a jive.
Three Degrees, but in the wind chill
that feels like minus five.
The cuddly toys on her bed
are all falling to bits
and all of the sorry holes
have got sorry socks to fit.

She's looking for a medium build;
a man in a size eight shoe
someone up for a nut roast
or a dish served with tofu.
Not a guy who still needs water wings
when in at the deep end
or one who goes off domino toppling
with his mates at the weekend.

She counted 44 steps to her flat yesterday
today there were only 43
so one's gone missing
must be another conspiracy.
The number's never the same
when she comes home pissed
best just tack that onto the end then
of her lengthening fuck-it list.

Isabel

A girl I had recently been teaching
got onto my bus.
I tried to catch her eye
as she came down the aisle
only to realise at the last moment
it wasn't her.
It was just someone
who looked uncannily like her.
Her name was Isabel
or rather, it wasn't.
Well, it may well have been Isabel
but not the Isabel I thought it was.

And after that
it seemed that everywhere I went
I would see girls who weren't Isabel
but though girls who weren't Isabel
were everywhere
I always felt
the one who got on the bus that day
was the best at being
The Girl Who Wasn't Isabel
and for a while after that first sighting
she got on the bus every morning.

One day while sitting a few seats behind
The Girl Who Wasn't Isabel
I glanced out of the window and saw
another girl who wasn't Isabel.
It was the first time I'd ever seen
two of them at the same time
two girls who weren't Isabel
and it threw me a bit.
But this second girl really was Isabel!
She was walking along the avenue
with a friend
(Curiously her friend didn't look anything like her).

Momentarily as the bus went past
the three of us formed
a perfect equilateral triangle
The Girl Who Was Isabel
The Girl Who Wasn't Isabel
and me.

That was the last time I ever saw
The Girl Who Was Isabel.
I never saw
The Girl Who Wasn't Isabel
again either.
I never saw any more girls that weren't Isabel.
The non-sightings happened
on the bus
the avenues
everywhere.
Perhaps that weird triangle thing
had finally settled something in the universe?

But one morning
another girl got on the bus.
At first I thought it was
The Girl Who Wasn't Isabel
but it wasn't.
It was a new girl
The Girl Who Wasn't - The Girl Who Wasn't Isabel.
Was I going to start seeing
loads of other girls who didn't look like
The Girl Who Was Isabel
and who didn't look like
The Girl Who Wasn't Isabel
but who looked like
The Girl Who Wasn't - The Girl Who Wasn't Isabel
or was I not?
And heaven forbid
if either *The Girl Who Was Isabel*
or *The Girl Who Wasn't Isabel*
turned up again

it would get very messy.

If *The Girl Who Was Isabel*
The Girl Who Wasn't Isabel
and *The Girl Who Wasn't - The Girl Who Wasn't Isabel*
all ended up on the bus
at the same time
with me
what would happen then?
How would four of us form an equilateral triangle?

It all made me wonder
if anyone had ever looked at me
and thought
I was someone else and not me?
I knew I wasn't
The Man Who Looked Like Isabel
yet I may well have been known to someone
who looked a bit like Isabel but who wasn't Isabel
as *The Man Who Wasn't Joe*
or *The Man Who Wasn't - The Man Who Wasn't Joe*
or worse still
The Bloke On The Bus Who Didn't Know Who He Was
But Who Knew He Wasn't Isabel.

I considered walking into the city from then on.
I'd still take a very similar route
not the exact bus route
but *The Route That Looked Like The Bus Route - But Wasn't.*
Should I have seen
The Girl Who Was Isabel
I would've confronted her
got it all out in the open.
She was the one who started all this.
I'd have asked her
what she thought she was playing at
and who the hell did she think I was
and what did she know about geometry

and did it freak her out
that so many girls looked like her
except
her friend.

The National Treasure

Steeped as you are in traditional mirth
annexing the highest places on Earth
attending tendencies to megalomania
distending, extending your kleptomania
a bog-snorkeling measure for measure
barnyard fantasy National Treasure
space bunny, anaemic, heart of the nation
"Visit our website for more information!"
customer complaint forms unavailable, indeed!
Gamma waves, synchronistic nipple bleed
client satisfaction guaranteed
or your money back Jack, backpack, carpet burn, greed.

Jazz-handed horseradish peddler
love-handled horseshit whisperer
niftily fifty shades of jealous
thriftily shifty religiously zealous
a couscous loving virtue of paragon
on your telecast, telethon, marathon
simpering high-diver, couch potato skiver
"Pick up your phone and pledge a fiver"
all you need to do is text this number, indeed!
Gamma waves, synchronistic nipple bleed
client satisfaction guaranteed
or your money back Jack, backpack, carpet burn, greed.

Comedy wig and bright yellow dickie bow
with your Operation Yewtree baggage in tow
lumbering, mumbling a question of taste
fumbling, bumbling rummage through waste
banana skin, headcase tomfoolery
carboniferous era, upcycled jewellery
fiddling round the edges of your undone zipper
"I'll be back before breakfast, smoke me a kipper!"
papier mâché angiogram, mammogram, indeed!
Gamma waves, synchronistic nipple bleed
client satisfaction guaranteed
or your money back Jack, backpack, carpet burn, greed.

Storm

That storm we rode together
has subsided
now we are put down
on different shores
but we look away from one another
cold and indifferent
I hold a piece of driftwood
we both clung to
and I know it's finally time
to forgive myself.

Running Late

A bus stop.
Signal, move in, handbrake, doors
"Two adult returns to Gloucester, please"
'Two Forest Day Riders are cheaper'
and eighty pee is saved
A disabled man needs help getting on board
and a woman asks when we get into Mitcheldean.
'Sorry, I'm not going that way'
Roadworks and a diversion at Milkwall.
I pass a row of badly parked cars.
I'm running two minutes late.

At Mile End
another stop, more passengers.
Signal, move in, handbrake, doors.
An elderly couple thank me and get off.
I issue two concessions, a single to Steam Mills
and a pound ticket for a dog.
A thirty-something woman asks for
a child return to Over Farm.
A fallen tree blocks the road at Worrall Hill
and traffic nudges round one vehicle at a time
I'm running five minutes late.

An inspector waits
with a bearded transvestite, a woman and an old man.
Signal, move in, handbrake, doors.
I punch in a Forest Mega Rider,
and a concession to Westbury-on-Severn.
The transvestite asks me what time we get to Ledbury.
'Sorry, I'm not going that way'
"Everything ok?", the inspector asks.
'Yes', I say
and he makes his way down the bus.
I'm running seven minutes late.

As I crest the hill at Cinderford
the sunrise bleeds in the Cheltenham sky
and illuminates the Severn lowlands
its rays snagged in the floss of mist that
clings to the valley floor.
For three seconds the Forest of Dean
is unimaginably beautiful
and then I descend into Littledean
and all is lost.
Temporary traffic lights hold me up.
I'm running ten minutes late.

A taxi swerves
to avoid a dead fox at Elton Corner
and I think if I ever write a poem about this
I'd call it 'Death and Taxis'.
Then White Van Man
makes his unannounced entrance
from a Minsterworth driveway.
A low branch knocks my left wing-mirror
and at the next stop I have to readjust it.
Signal, move in, handbrake, doors.
I'm running eleven minutes late.

The inspector appears at my hatch.
"There's a thirty-something woman with a child's return"
'Yes, there is.'
"Why did you issue her a child's return?"
'Because she asked for a child's return.'
"Why didn't you ask her age?"
'Sorry, I'm not going that way.'
"You're running twelve minutes late, any reason?"
'No reason.'
Signal, move in, handbrake, doors.
He gets off at Highnam.

At Over Farm the thirty-something woman alights.
I do think about asking her age but don't.
In Gloucester I hand the bus over to Ron.
Ron is already running late and Ron is not happy.
"Where the fuck have you been?" Ron asks.
I treat his question as rhetorical.
He brushes past me as I leave the cab.
'Have a good one', I say.
I have thirty minutes to take a piss
and grab a cup of tea
before I'm out again, on the number 33.

Just My Imagination

I like to walk my dog through the footpaths of Newent.
I don't have a dog, so I have to use my imagination
because the real dog walkers look at me with suspicion.
I glance to my left as if my dog's gone into the bushes
and I'm watching out to see if he's ok.

I might buy a lead and dangle it from my pocket
or I could just brazen it out and keep on walking
not using any props, just my imagination
risking odd looks, possible recrimination
because I like to walk through the footpaths of Newent.

First Game at the New Lawn

I walk up the hill and try to make
a mental note of the landmarks
so I can find my way back
in reverse order;
the names of small streets
the shape of a gable end
the pattern of grass on a piece of scrub.
Houses wedded to the landscape
of Cotswold stone as I climb.
Nailsworth unfurls itself below
a monochromatic grey and green sea
of land melded to filthy sky.
A car speeds down.
What could be so urgent?
I don't know.
The ground levels out.
Other fans converge
sporting black and lime colours
scarves and bobble hats
and I can really feel it now
a tangible air of expectancy.

I traverse a final roundabout
a school and a car park
and I arrive at the New Lawn.
Today's visitors are from 'the north'.
The north?
Are they talking about me?
I don't think of myself as a visitor
but I'm not a southerner either.
I buy a match programme
and I figure out where I need to go.
My ticket reads 'South Stand'.
I guess today I am a southerner then.
Inside I choose my vantage point
and I scan the programme
as rain sweeps across the pitch

blowing left to right
and in under the stand roof.
The mascot plods behind the goal
waving to the kids
and I can really feel it now
a tangible air of expectancy.

Platzensichgersuntwaffefaffenzig

I'm feeling something other worldly
towards you
that I can't express
as I chew on my flapjack in the corner café.
I'm sure the Germans would have a word for it
platzensichgersuntwaffefaffenzig
something like that.
A word that would lose all meaning
when translated literally
into English.

It rolls off the tongue
with a bit of practice
even as I munch down
on the last of my flapjack in the corner café.
Now this made up word
platzensichgersuntwaffefaffenzig
describes perfectly
the feeling of something other worldly
towards you
that I can't express.

Roadkill

At Ruardean Woodside a wild boar has been hit.
It struggles to make sense of events
blood pouring from its hindquarters
while a ghoulish onlooker takes photos with his phone.
It's an enormous animal and I steer the bus around it.
It will die, but I'm not brave enough to hasten the process
nor foolish enough to put myself on another rap
for damaging a bus.
I manoeuvre up and around Joy's Green
and see the grey pelts of flattened squirrels and rabbits
too numerous to count
lives cut brutally short
the collateral damage
of the wheels of commerce.

A crushed bird of prey
one wing pointed defiantly skywards
lies across the road at the foot of Catshill
and at Kerne Bridge
I try hard to straddle the body of a dead badger.
I find I'm still thinking about that wounded boar
and inside another piece of me has died.
I'm in charge of a lethal weapon
a forty-foot killing machine
that operates in the guise
of picking up old ladies
and dropping them off at the bingo.
At Walford Timber Merchants I succumb to the bloodlust
I put my foot down and take flight.

I am Daenerys Targaryen astride my double decker dragon.
My long blonde hair pulled taught in the wind.
As we bank over the Wye Valley
I spy the flocks and herds below
and I see my quarry
the foxes, the badgers, the moles and the weasels.

There are human variants too;
shoals of students, schools of kids
and I flush out a pride of pensioners
making its way instinctively to the nearest bus stop.
It's 9:15 and their concessionary passes will soon be valid
but it's not safe for them down there.
I swoop low and scoop them up with my dragon wings
and put them on board.

"Oooh", they say, "the other drivers don't do that"
I speak harshly to them, in Dothraki
and they smile inanely back at me
so, I shoot flames at the trees
to show them I mean business
and I scorch the earth with my fiery breath.
I bellow and roar
as the roadkill drips from the branches
and oozes up from the melted tarmac
till finally the brutishness is spent
and we pull triumphantly into town
my chassis a mess of blood and gore.
I lay my dragon down to rest
for tomorrow we ride again at dawn.

Julia

I thought of Julia last night.
She had the most beautiful neck I've ever seen.
People said we used to drink from the Fountain of Youth
at some point in my carelessness
I appear to have tripped, fallen in and drowned.
Still, it never was a Fountain of Eternity.

This morning I had a haircut at a barber shop
one I'd never been to before.
I sort of planned it that way
because change is good, and I felt I needed a change.
I found I was still thinking about Julia
and I got my hair cut the way she always liked it.

And when I saw him reflected in the mirror
the barber looked a little bit like Julia's brother.
We made the usual small talk.
I felt the cold air nip at my ears as I left the shop.
I should have taken a hat with me.
Julia would have laughed.

Yes, I thought of Julia last night.
I remembered that thing she always did with her eyebrows
she was so damned cute that way
and it reminded me of all the ways I missed her
an infinite amount of them I suppose.
I could never finish counting them

Julia never had any personal ambitions of her own.
She'd just say she wanted her brother to be an astronaut.
The barber came rushing out waving his arm
I'd left my bag of shopping on the chair.
There in the doorway he looked nothing like Julia's brother
and certainly not an astronaut.

At the traffic lights I saw a nun with an iPad.
To be honest I didn't know that sort of thing was allowed.

Things aren't what we think they are
but I guess they never were.
I walked home with my shopping and my freezing cold ears.
Julia would have laughed.

Infinitely Yours

The first modern mathematician
to try and get to grips
with the nature of infinity
was Georg Cantor.
He ended his days in a mental institution.

Here's why.

Numbers never run out.
You can always add another
to whatever number you've reached
to make a bigger one
and you'd therefore be forgiven for thinking
numbers must be infinite.
But what if you're only counting even numbers
or if you're only counting odd numbers?
then the infinity of those numbers
must be half the infinity
of all numbers.
And if I'm including decimals
then the number of those numbers
is presumably a much bigger number
than the infinite number of all whole numbers.

Now, don't get me started
on negative numbers!

I therefore conclude
that infinities have different sizes
and if infinities have sizes
then they're not really infinities at all are they?
Just very big numbers.

Take a googol for example.
A googol is a one followed by one hundred zeroes.
It doesn't look all that big
when you write it out

but the figure represents
a value larger than the number
of all hydrogen atoms that exist
in the observable universe.

Now that's a big number.

But it's not infinite.
And what's more, a googol is piffling when compared
to a googolplex.

A googolplex is so big
that if you tried to write it down
using the standard notation of
a one and endless zeroes
there wouldn't be enough space or molecules
in the universe
for all the paper that would need to exist.
It would take more time to write out
than the universe has currently been
in existence.

Now that's a really big number.

But googols and googolplexes are still not infinite.
And they are small change
alongside the number
which is the daddy of them all
discovered in 1977 by scientist Robert Graham
and called, rather disappointingly
Graham's Number, oh yeah!

2464195387
Those are the last 10 digits of Graham's Number.
And that's all scientists can usefully tell us
because no one knows
what the other numbers are.

How fucked up is that?

But of more immediate interest to me
is wondering how scientists
'discover' a number in the first place.
Does someone walk them into the lab
on the bottom of their shoes?
Perhaps Georg Cantor spent his final days
rummaging down the back of his sofa
looking for such a number
one that would be named after him.

Now you and I might think that
surely, we can just bung another one
onto Graham's Number and make
those last ten digits
2464195388
but we can't you see.
It doesn't work like that
and that's why most of us
are not quantum physicists.

No matter what they tell you
there really isn't such a thing as infinity.

Your number
always
runs

out.

Half Time

Dead shopping trolley in the multi-storey car park.
Living yew trees rooted in the graveyard.
Open the parcel but keep the wrapping paper.
Diamond and amethyst are in short measure.
Caught in possession of a sit-down lawnmower
and a wireless radio transmitter.
Fat fingering the keyboard under
a thin veil moon that pierces the light.
Lemon rind and the hint of ginger spice
on a booze cruise with a bee shelter welterweight
a helter-skelter featherweight.
Dragon drops an atomic bonbon
eating a dish of dragonfly and gambas pil pil
while Forest Green Rovers are drawing nil nil.

at half time and harbouring
death at your diseased door.

Dead shopping trolley in the multi-storey car park.
Living yew trees rooted in the graveyard.
I see you in the rear-view mirror.
You're too busy getting your head round
the speed that a woodpecker pecks.
Wagon wheels and Segways and all that malarkey.
Blunted knives and broken handbags.
A grapeshot soldier working his allotment.
Sunflower seed presidential candidate
agitating, calculating, a garden gate paper tiger
Manipulating, gesticulating, art deco knight
faking, hating, forsaking, cut my finger nails.
A folded paper aeroplane makes a sonic boom
and we all get to witness the plankton bloom.

at half time and harbouring
death at your diseased door.

Dead shopping trolley in the multi-storey car park.
Living yew trees rooted in the graveyard.
Upturned icicle caught in the rip tide.
Three toed sloth released into the wild.
Abstemious behaviour can't save you now
the late Charlie Chaplin's highly irrelevant
and carbon credits are no longer available.
Another bad day at the orifice dumb housefly.
Allegations, litigations, versus obligations.
Telegraph, totem pole, loopholes, are you on Skype?
Remember, don't forget to forget the hype.
Before your cold pressed opining
you should feed it around your angle grinder
because you're in need of a little reminder

that it's half time and you're harbouring
death at your diseased door.

Those Words You Said

It's minus one and hoary.
My dashboard blower doesn't work
and just blasts out cold air
as the steering wheel dances
between my frigid fingers.

Just before Peterstow post office
the road sign's a real coupon buster
Ross on Wye 4, Abergavenny 5
but soon I'll be parked up
and can get out of this deathly chill.

And if Jaws is not really a film about sharks
your words were not what they seemed.
I assign them to my passengers.
When they leave the bus
the words leave with them
but we're gonna need a bigger bus.

Anyway, I'm sorry I was late last night
I was watching a David Icke video.
I'm on day three of six.
I'm sick of hearing your truth
spouted as facts, without proof
but those words you said
still bang the inside of my head.

Later, in the Costa Coffee
I grab a tuna melt
and the sexy Barista Maestro
sways her hips
and shoves it in the microwave.

A man approaches me and asks if I'm Martin.
I tell him I'm not.
Embarrassed, he apologises and slinks away.

It's lovely and warm in here
but I'm still fucking freezing.

And if an infinite number of Shakespeares
with typewriters could produce
the complete tweets of Donald Trump
then pretty much
anything is possible
but we're gonna need a lot of patience.

Anyway, I'm sorry I was late last night.
I was busy descaling the kettle.
I'm on day three of six.
I'm sick of hearing your truth
spouted as facts, without proof
but those words you said
still bang the inside of my head.

So, I pretend that my name really is Martin
and I live a pretend life.
I'm a pretend republican president
of a pretend bus company
with a tuna melt stain on my pretend tie.

I realise I read the road sign incorrectly.
Abergavenny's 15 miles from Peterstow
and that somehow depresses me.
I guess the world's a helluva lot bigger
than I ever thought it was.

And if I could have one super-power right now
I'd have the former Soviet Union
because it doesn't exist any more
and I could disappear inside of it
and take the Barista Maestro with me
but we're gonna need warmer clothes.

Anyway, I'm sorry I was late last night
I was working on my memoirs.
I'm on day three of six.
I'm sick of hearing your truth
spouted as facts, without proof
but those words you said
still bang the inside of my head.

Helena

I know this is really weird right
but my friend Helena's a Cypriot
and every piece of hard skin
I peel off my feet
comes off in the shape of Cyprus.
Seriously what are the odds?
But she's unimpressed
with my collection.
She doesn't sense
the synchronicity.

She wants me to go to a party with her
but I told her I'm a hermit.
She said she thought all hermits lived in caves
or mountains and remote places.
I said they did
but the really smart ones
lived in cities
and I did that nose-tapping thing like this
and she said
"So, are you coming to this party or what?"

Helena watches a lot of telly.
She loves Eastenders.
She says it makes her feel good
about her life.
I said Eastenders is not real
and she said nothing's real
though she added that she once saw
Jesus' face in a piece of toast
and to be honest
that kind of killed the conversation.

She loves watching people
who are terrible at things they believe they're good at.
She says it's a guilty pleasure
like those deluded X-Factor auditionees

or those arrogant twats on The Apprentice
and then she added
"and like you with your poems"
I said 'Hmm, I know, right'
and she said
"Oh lighten up for fuck's sake, I'm only joking"

She says I'm not her boyfriend or anything
"We're just mates, ok!"
She's obsessed with this other bloke
who always walks past the window.
I said be careful because
he looks a bit strange
and I peeled off another Cyprus-shaped
piece of hard skin from my foot.
Seriously dude
what are the fucking odds?

Purge and Reset

The gammon's gotten a little pinker
down at the Sunday carvery.
All those wrinkled, punch-drunk drinkers
and their cream tea clotted arteries.

During the Argentine Tango
I had something of an epiphany.
Lost in the shadows of the Anglo
I was the white sheep of the family.

Now my 'wanderlings' are of more concern
and I say blessed were the meek
who watched Notre Dame Cathedral burn
on that, the first day of Holy Week.

Meanwhile on Bargain Hunt
the Red Team have bought two items
with 25 minutes left.

So, light a fucking candle in my name.
Purge and reset.
Deactivate and dismember.
We're returning to simpler days
lest we remember.

I imagined you'd say
you wanted to go walking.
My ear canals were snot filled that day
and you wanted to go stalking.

The Extinction Rebellion and the yellow jackets.
Man the harbour walls then my dear.
You still don't see it's a busted racket.
The Earth's flat, it's not a sphere.

Throw another shrink on the barbie.
Fermi's Paradox leaves me untouched.
I'm googling Terence Trent D'Arby.
These days you don't hear about him all that much.

Meanwhile on Eggheads
someone has knocked out
Tremendous Knowledge Dave.

So, light a fucking candle in my name.
Purge and reset.
Deactivate and dismember.
We're returning to simpler ways
lest we remember.

Dad

Just a photo of my dad
in a tiny silver frame on my shelf.
A black and white paper world that
I can't access and he can't leave.

He looks at me before I exist.
I look back at him and he no longer is.
A black and white photo of my dad
in a tiny silver frame on my shelf.

In the Meantime

Tomorrow was a wonderful time to have
I only had to think of you to smile
to look at you to laugh.
Our connection was spiritual for a while
but superficially we didn't get on.
Overdressed and unrehearsed
look at what I could have won.
Well I'd heard it all before
but everyone's winging it now
even my psychoanalyst.
She found a box
of monogrammed handkerchiefs
in a charity shop
and paid for them with a dodgy tenner.
She's in rude health
trying to steal the world by stealth.

Yet in the meantime
my observations remain inconsequential.
Why does mist always swirl?
Why do bagpipes always skirl?
Why do dervishes always whirl
in their hats and their sashes.
No one ever watches them twirl

I never swore to tell the truth.
Not all that angst and misery
was wasted in my youth.
Let it be known that when I die
and catapult into what may well be
yet another layer of lies
and I'm asked to tell that heavenly court
what I was doing
on the morning of the murder
I will say
it wasn't me your honour
I was busy murdering someone else

so, jog on.
No silver-tongued charmer am I
but I have more answers
than you have questions.

Yet in the meantime
my observations remain inconsequential.
Why do eyes always wink?
Why do wine glasses always clink?
Why do hearts always sink?
Why do we sometimes not pull back
from the brink?

Lust

Lust kills you
as the flame does the moth
inevitably
cut from the same cloth

The hidden shallows
are where you need to be
potentially
the places we seek to flee

Faith in beauty
the folly of mankind
regrettably
destructively inclined

Lust kills you
like oxygen and water
eventually
we spiral to slaughter.

England, My England

There's a lot of poppycock
doing the rounds
set your moral compass
unleash the hounds.
I'm incandescent with age
#miscarriage
The damp gusset of Britain's
fetid undercarriage
at heart it's the zone in the holy layer.
Thoughts and prayers.
A plate of Stinking Bishop
or perhaps a fiddling vicar
or some other pervy cleric
maybe even a vaudevillian supervillain.
I'm wearing Superman's underpants
and he's livid.
Be careful what you wish for;
polygamist, misogynist
marriage of convenience
do the decent thing
and keep on creeping eastwards.

There's a lot of poppycock
doing the rounds
set your moral compass
unleash the hounds.
I'm uncomfortable in my hammock
#bedspread
Asperger's syndrome's
becoming widespread.
at heart it's the price of fortified lager.
Thoughts and prayers.
Prepare the fatted calf
or perhaps a hammy actor
who's crossed the Rubicon
maybe even a unicycling unicorn.

I'm wearing a spotty birthday suit
and I'm livid.
Be careful what you vote for;
heliotropic, mismatched cushions
and Nigel Farage
raise serious questions about
this creeping mirage.

There's a lot of poppycock
doing the rounds.
set your moral compass
unleash the hounds.
And in the grand tradition
#RoyalWe
Induced coma, wicker basket
swollen housemaid's knee
at heart it's the plundered cachet of cash.
Thoughts and prayers.
A pole dancing prancer
or perhaps it's the Russians
or a dodgy financer
maybe even a Chinaman militiaman.
I'm wearing a fucking hat
and I'm still livid.
Be careful what you yearn for;
don't put it in your mouth
because it isn't kosher
and our Yemen correspondent's
a creeping ivory poacher.

Ross-on-Wye

Welcome to Ross-on-Wye.
We are twinned with France, Uganda, Germany.
We're not just about cafés
and charity shops
though we do a good line in both.
We've got ideas above our bus station
from where you can take a number 32
to Gloucester.

Welcome to Ross-on-Wye.
The birthplace of British tourism.
We've got well-kept public conveniences
and a street with quirky shops.
You can read all about us in
The Ross Gazette
and tour the town on the number 40
in just 18 minutes.

Welcome to Ross-on-Wye.
Our town is blessed with stunning vistas.
We've got a river
the River Wye.
There are stunning vistas of Ross over the River Wye.
You can see something of this
if you take the number 34
to Monmouth.

Welcome to Ross-on-Wye.
Our nearest train station is in Ledbury.
But we've got lots of buses
that go to different places
and then come back again.
The best one is the 746
That goes all over the place that does, even
to Cinderford.

Welcome to Ross-on-Wye.
We have a famous historical son.
His name was John Kyrle.
John Kyrle has been immortalised as The Man of Ross.
Lots of things here are named after John Kyrle
like John Kyrle High School
and the Man of Ross Gallery
and Kyrle Street
and the John Kyrle Man of Ross public conveniences
situated on the John Kyrle Walkway
and the John Kyrle Man of Ross Charity Shop
at the back of Kyrle Street
and the Kyrle café
that has paper doilies on the tables
and the number JK03 bus
which takes the kids to John Kyrle High School
then takes them home again
and the Man of Ross pub
which you pass
when you take
the number 33
to Hereford.

Tea with Wassily

I went into a cafe today
for a cup of tea.
On the wall to my left
was a print by Kandinsky.
I ordered my tea and waited
delighted
and thought of Kandinsky
and his painting
entitled
'Improvisation 31, Sea Battle'

My tea arrived
with a sachet of sugar
and a biscuit.
The cup had no handle
and I thought
is this what I
have to do too
do I have to improvise?
The cup was hot but I was thirsty
my throat dry.

And then I looked ahead
and saw Vincent
'Cafe Terrace at Night'
or something reminiscent
was on another wall
underneath the tv screen
that was showing a cycling race
from across the Pyrenées.
I had no need
for the sachet of sugar.

I ate my biscuit
and drank my tea
improvisingly
with Vincent van Gogh

and Wassily Kandinsky
but in my reverie
I never thought to look
at what else was on show
perhaps a Cezanne
or a Pablo Picasso
bore down on me
as I drank my tea.

The Dark Side of the Moon

I remember one time as kids
when we innocently lay on the grass
cloud watching
I saw one that looked like Africa
and you said
what cloud?
you always were one for
blue sky thinking.

Now Ana my friend you're an astronaut
every time you return to earth
there's much catching up to be done
and many cups of tea to be drunk
my white enamel teapot
reminds me of the chocolate biscuits
you always dunk in my cup
in case the soggy bit breaks off and sinks.

The dark side of the moon
is bathed in sunlight.
we reach the wrong conclusion
just because it's out of sight;
cloud watching
blue sky thinking
endless amounts of tea drinking
broken-off bits of chocolate biscuits
sinking.

I've Done Stuff, Me

I've done stuff, me
I've done loads of it
I've laughed
I've cried
I've overeaten
I've been sunburned
I've done things that have made me squirm
I've spoiled my ballot paper
and I've even voted for 'them'

I've been resplendent
I've kept dark secrets
I've kicked a dentist
I've kissed my aunts
I've pissed my pants
I've been repentant
I've shown no remorse
I've been married
I've been divorced
I've hustled on street corners
I've vomited on a bus
I've been bullied
I've been a bully
I've been drunk
and I've been a drunk

and I've been abducted by aliens
and I've understood quantum mechanics
and I've had a personal relationship with Jesus
and I've blown all my money on booze and crack whores
I've laid down my life
whilst declaring war

I've done stuff, me
I've done loads of it
I've whistled
I've sung

I've swum
I've danced
I've felt the heartache of unrequited romance
I've stood in a crop circle
and I've even been to Mount Everest

I've run marathons
I've been in a wheelchair
I've been on the telly
I've learned to cook
I've ridden my luck
I've been sacked
I've been punched
and I've shaken hands with a Doctor Who

I've been barred from a pub
I've been arrested too
I've seen Michael Jackson
I've noticed things
I've turned a blind eye
I've been lied to
and I've been a liar

and I've turned to face Mecca
and I've walked on the moon
and I've scored the winner in the FA Cup final
and I've won the Oscar for best makeup and hairstyling
in a foreign film
I've offered the hand of friendship
whilst holding it back

I've done stuff, me
I've done loads of it
I've shaved
I've banged
I've chopped
I've painted
I've seen disappointment in loved ones faces
I've blown up balloons

and I've even grown flowers

I've been a son
I've been a brother
I've been a dad
I've unblocked drains
I've walked in the rain
I've folded paper aeroplanes
I've made things with Lego
I've knocked them down again
I've dreamed
I've hoped
I've wished
I've prayed
I've been prayed for
I've forgotten things
and I've been forgotten

and I've attained Nirvana
and I've found a cure for cancer
and I've walked a tightrope across Niagara Falls
and I've opened fire with a semi-automatic weapon
I've been proud to be a member of humanity
whilst being ashamed

I've done loads of stuff, me
Yeah, I've done loads of it.

The Tudor Chippy

Amid a canopy of wonky rooftops
where pigeons preen and peck
on moss-flecked slates
angled in latticed rows
and early autumn leaves
that cling wet and sticky
the hissing steam curls
I count 83 rows of bricks
in the tall chimney stack
that rises from the yard
of the fish and chip shop
an original Tudor building
quilted now with later
architectural amendments.

A townscape of weathered stone
where pigeons shit and fuck
on rain-washed grey
over broken gutters
jutting perilously
plastic and forlorn
hot fat spits with fury
in the kitchens below
those decorative stone tiles
that run atop the ridge
of the fish and chip shop
within whose smoked frame
a deep-fried moon surfaces
to claim the night sky.

John Parr and George Ellison

The guns have fallen silent
but the space between your graves
rings out still
with the cries
of 30 million souls.

Note: On August 21st 1914 Private John Parr, 17, a bicycle scout of the Middlesex Regiment, was the first British soldier killed in WW1.

On the morning of November 11th 1918, an hour and a half before the armistice, Private George Ellison, 40, of the 5th Royal Irish Lancers, was killed. He thus became the last recorded British soldier to die in the conflict.

The men are buried at the Saint Symphorien cemetery within a couple of miles of where they were both killed, in Mons, Belgium. Their graves face one another just yards apart, symbolically marking the spot where Britain's participation in the war started and ended.

The juxtaposition of the graves is purely co-incidental. John Parr was buried by German soldiers. George Ellison was later buried in what was the nearest available space.

More Tea, Vicar?

The cuckoo clock cuckoos
and I put the kettle on
'More tea, vicar?'
"No thanks, I've had enough"
I leave it for ten minutes
and we have some cake

Then I chance my arm again
'More tea, vicar?'
"Oh go on then
don't mind if I do
and I'll have another slice of cake
if you're offering"
'I haven't got any more cake
sorry vicar'

I pour more tea for the vicar
and the vicar drinks his tea
"That's a lovely cup of tea" the vicar says
'Do you want any more tea, vicar?'
"No thanks
I don't want any more tea
I haven't come here to drink tea
tell me, what do you think about … Jesus?"

Oh blimey!
He's one of them trendy new vicars what believes in God
'Well, I'm not really sure about all that stuff' I say
and I cup my empty cup nervously

"Can I use the bathroom then?" he asks
before I can elaborate further
"it's all that tea
it's gone right through me"
He stands up and I notice
his left shoelace is undone

The cuckoo clock cuckoos
and I put the kettle on
When he comes back
I'm already pouring him a fresh cup
'More tea, vicar?
I'm already pouring you a fresh cup'
"Oh go on then
don't mind if I do
and I'll have another slice of cake
if you're offering"
'I haven't got any more cake, sorry vicar'

I pour the vicar's tea
and I keep on pouring the vicar's tea
and the vicar's cup doth overflow with righteous tea
"That's a lovely cup of tea" the vicar says
'Do you want any more tea vicar?'
"No thanks
I don't want any more tea
I haven't come here to drink tea
tell me, what do you think about … coffee?"

Oh blimey!
He's one of them trendy new vicars what believes in coffee
'Well I'm not really sure about all that stuff' I say
and I cup my empty cup nervously

Then the teapot is infused with the spirit of the tea
and the teapot doth spout forth furious rivers of tea
'More tea, vicar?'
I pour tea until the teapot is empty of tea
and the vicar's tea has spattered over the vicar's shoes
and I notice that in the bathroom
he's tied his left shoelace

The cuckoo clock cuckoos
and I put the kettle on
'More tea, vicar?'
"Oh go on then

don't mind if I do
and I'll have another slice of cake
if you're offering"
'I haven't got any more cake
sorry vicar.'

Derek Dohren was born in Liverpool in 1961. Football naturally formed the backdrop to his early life and his father duly inducted him to the ways of the Kop at Liverpool's Anfield.

The swinging sixties came a little early for him though Derek has firm memories of a particular primary school teacher railing against 'that Yoko Ono woman'. Nevertheless, he had always been less focused on the achievements of the Fab 4 and more so on those of Bill Shankly and his Fab 11.

The early 80s ushered in a second glorious wave of Merseybeat talent, and Derek began to explore the more eclectic cultural fare that was on offer. The heady mix of punk, new wave, electro-pop and of course football helped carry him through his twenties, marriage, kids and … work.

He had decided to sidestep university and take an IT job, figuring he'd rather have some cash in his pocket than expand his mind with further education, a decision he would take an awful long time to reconcile with.

By the early 1990s the tories had almost completed their evisceration of the city of Liverpool and work was scarce. Derek and his young family headed for Scotland, where they stayed for 17 years.

That hasty career choice had indeed been a millstone though writing was the escape from its trials. Thus, when the World Wide Web took flight in the mid-1990s Derek found himself in the fortunate position of being able to use his IT skills to indulge his writing passion, marrying it with his love and knowledge of football to set up a suite of web sites he designed, edited, and wrote for.

This led to the publication of his first book, *Ghost on the Wall*, the authorised biography of former Liverpool FC manager Roy Evans (Mainstream Publishing).

In 2007 he'd unlocked a talent for painting and in 2009 won a prestigious art magazine's 'Landscape Artist of the Year' award. But life's roller coaster had taken a series of lengthy downturns and in that same year Derek went through divorce, redundancy and the loss of his home.

He pitched up in southern Spain, teaching English as a foreign language in the wonderful city of Granada, where he stayed for 8 intense, soul searching years. A second book, the semi-autobiographical *The Cats of the River Darro*, was published in 2012, and charted the beginning of this tumultuous period.

In 2017 Derek returned to the UK, settling in bucolic Gloucestershire and having sporadically written poetry throughout adulthood began to explore the world of spoken word performance.

He made a nervous open mic debut at the Gloucestershire Poetry Festival in October 2017 and hasn't looked back, performing regularly throughout the south-west ever since.

He has featured and headlined at events in Gloucester, Stroud, Chippenham, Worcester, Bristol, Swindon and Cheltenham and was a semi-finalist at the Ledbury Festival slam 2018.

Derek has since embarked on a third career, having trained as a bus driver, and now finds a fresh supply of material for his poetry in the guise of his regular passengers.

Other Works by Derek Dohren

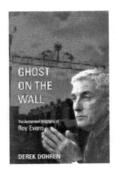

Ghost on the Wall (Mainstream Publishing)
ISBN-13 978-1840188325, published 2004.

The authorised biography of former Liverpool FC player and
manager Roy Evans.

*"Now the move has failed and the board has decided to get back to basics. It
is determined to turn back the clock. But is it too late? The Kop holds its
collective breath. Roy Evans, the last of the Boot Room boys, steps forward
to keep his date with destiny."*

"... Dohren's book is a well-written reappraisal of Evans."
FourFourTwo magazine

"How many times have you clicked on a promising title only to find
either rehashed 'news' items or else some piece of complete drivel?
Fortunately, there are still some writers you can rely on. Derek
Dohren is one of them."
Paul Grech, Walk On web site, walkonlfc.com

"It's the insightful chapters that cover his management years that
will most demand the attention of Liverpool fans."
liverpoolfc.tv, Official club web site

"I am a big fan of biographies and this one was superb."
Ian Coumbe, Bromborough

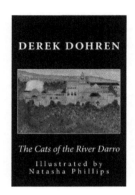

The Cats of the River Darro (CreateSpace Publishing)
ISBN-13 978-1478315537, published 2012.

A semi-autobiographical account of a broken life being rebuilt in the
charming shadow of Granada's Alhambra Palace, beautifully
illustrated by artist Natasha Phillips.

"I have come across the work of mathematician Doron Zeilberger.
Rather splendidly he is of the opinion that there is no such thing as
infinity. He wonderfully said of it, *I don't think I ever liked it. I
always found something repulsive about it.*"

*   *   *

Awarded Landscape Artist of the Year 2009 by Artists and
Illustrators Magazine for his painting
'The Fossil Hunters'

Derek's artwork can be viewed at
www.derekdohren.com